In the
Land of Milk
and Honey

by
Joyce Carol Thomas

Illustrated by
Floyd Cooper

Amistad
An Imprint of HarperCollinsPublishers

Amistad is an imprint of HarperCollins Publishers.

In the Land of Milk and Honey
Text copyright © 2012 by Joyce Carol Thomas
Illustrations copyright © 2012 by Floyd Cooper
All rights reserved. Manufactured in China.
No part of this book may be used or reproduced in any manner whatsoever without
written permission except in the case of brief quotations embodied in critical articles
and reviews. For information address HarperCollins Children's Books, a division of
HarperCollins Publishers, 10 East 53rd Street, New York, NY 10022.
www.harpercollinschildrens.com

Library of Congress Cataloging-in-Publication Data is available.
ISBN 978-0-06-025383-7 (trade bdg.)

Typography by Carla Weise
12   13   14   15   16   SCP   10   9   8   7   6   5   4   3   2   1
❖
First Edition

For my beautiful new great-granddaughter, Maxine
—J.C.T.

For Joyce
—F.C.

The waiting train huffs
"Hurry, hurry, hurry!"
And I worry, worry, worry
Hissing wheels
hiss, hiss, hiss
and I'm afraid we'll
miss, miss, miss
the train!

Then the whistle sounds long and lonesome
and the conductor sings
"All aboard!"

I ease myself back in the window seat
and breathe in
as the train breathes out
We're on our way!
On our way
to the Land of Milk and Honey

Daddy says,
"If the lemons are big as oranges
if the oranges are big as grapefruits
if you bite into a strawberry
and taste heaven in your mouth
why, you're in California
the Land of Milk and Honey."

Mama says,
"If the redwoods are tall as giants
if golden bears fish like men
and quail fly higher than eagles
you know you're in
the Land of Milk and Honey."

And so we ride into early afternoon
past quick and slow-stepping lizards
basking hood-eyed
on dazzling rocks

We ride into late afternoon
past a snake whose body is a pen
writing calligraphy
on the paper-dry earth

We ride into dusky evening
past a cactus raising
hairy arms to catch the
last light from the falling sun

My brothers play marbles
in the middle of the aisle
They're jittery things, skittering
and hiding under Mama's feet
Their tiger eyes
surprising two men playing dominoes

    The train lurches
    and sends them spinning back
    staring marble-eyed at me

        My sister unwraps
        a chopped egg sandwich
        I wash my half down
        with Grapette soda pop
        the bottle streaked with marbles of cold

In the morning
I wake up early enough to see California
spreading its sands of welcome
and I catch the
desert dance of
a coyote chasing a rabbit
through tumbling sagebrush

Now the sand turns to rich earth
Up and down the windy valley
migrant workers sweating through red bandannas
run up and down the rows
carrying boxes of tomatoes
on their heads
Not one falls

Up and down the windy valley
grape cutters shaded by green vines
cut red grapes from their stalks

Freeing pungent aromas and mariachi songs
out into the atmosphere
until they make the air delicious
Up and down the windy valley
workers in the onion fields
unbend their backs
to wave back at me
smiling on the traveling train
And I'm glad I'm here

Finally
we reach the city
where the ships sit
anchored in the coastal waters
like iron mountains
docked in the bay

"Look at the people!" I whisper
and mimic the rustling way
folks swish down the street
in the fine design of their clothes

Look at the people!
And their fascinating faces
Look at the people!
All ages, all races

At the welcome party
limber-legged dancers
shimmy in and out of each other's arms
And ever-changing rhythms
call the feet to follow the beat
here in
this Land of Milk and Honey

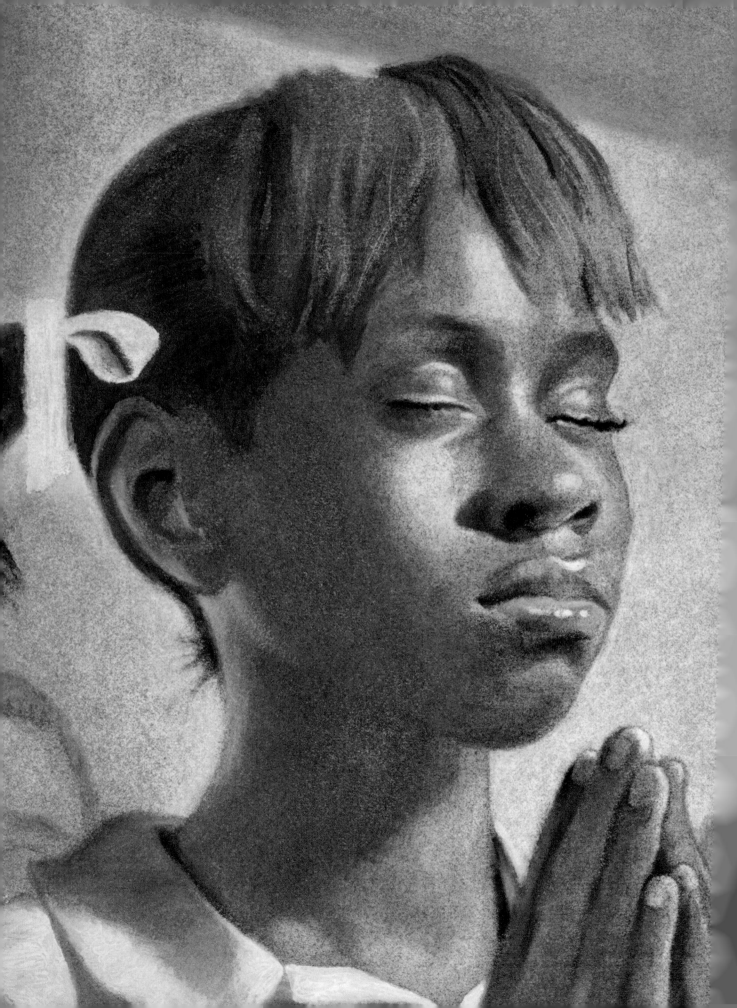

In the old mission building
arched in tile and stucco
I sing in the stained-glass choir
where the music swings
and every voice rings
with its own true sound
Oh, listen! Can't you hear the harmony?
Here in the Land
the Land of Milk and Honey

In Ginger's Restaurant
Mama pours hot milk
into mugs of shaved chocolate
then swizzles in cinnamon sticks
"A Mexican concoction," she explains

At the next table
a couple share jasmine tea in
a steaming glass

Across the street
a boy tears African bread
his fingers sopping it in peanut stew

I lean over and take another sip
of my luxurious drink
When everything I taste seems
spoon-sweetened with honey
an "Ummm" escapes my mouth

Beyond the bay
mountains topped with ice cream snow
rise
reaching toward the cloud-powdered sky
in the Land of Milk and Honey

Here
cool blue ocean pacifies the eyes
Soothing waves
foamy as milk
seem to sing
"Stay
stay here with us
here, here in the Land of Milk and Honey."

And we stay

AUTHOR'S NOTE

I moved to California from Oklahoma in 1948. During that time, many people made the journey west, where the quality of light was special and the weather was warmer year-round, the flowers brighter and the grass greener.

My aunt Corine was one of the first in my family to make the journey. On January 2, 1936, when she was twenty years old, she left Oklahoma for Southern California. She was there in 1941 when the U.S. entered World War II. She worked as a riveter in the Lockheed Aircraft plant and at Moore's Dry Dock Shipyard—both jobs that until then would have been held by men. By 1943, she moved north to the Bay Area and lived near my other two aunts, Aunt Annie Mae and Aunt Birdtee.

In 1948, my mother took ill and needed my aunts' help with her many children. So my father, who worked as a Pullman porter for Southern Pacific Railroad, booked my mother, sister, younger brothers, and me passage on the train from Oklahoma to California. After we were safely aboard, my father and my older brothers drove our Oldsmobile west.

At the time we entered the state, California was so spread out that miles of fruit and nut trees and acres of asparagus and hayfields rolled between cities and towns. Where we lived on a chicken ranch, tomato fields grew right up to our back door.

Now the mountains have been cut through to make way for freeways, the forests cut into smaller parcels, and the hills and valleys crowded with new houses built so close together there is little space for strawberry fields or walnut groves.

Yet the quality of light remains, and so does the vital and warm spirit of my California neighbors. While farmers may no longer plant acres of crops, today fruit trees, flowers, and vegetable gardens grow in our backyards and on our decks. Since riding that train in 1948, I continue to live here in this golden state near my family and make it my home.

I often focus on the joy and possibility reflected here in the California faces of people of all races, cultures, and ethnicities who journeyed to live here. I'm glad my family came to California. In this welcoming state, so many have decided to make a life, filled with freedom, plenty, and opportunity.

I'm glad to be among them, here in this Land of Milk and Honey.

—Joyce Carol Thomas
Berkeley, California